Animals
A To Z

T. J. Garrett

ACKNOWLEDGMENTS

This book is dedicated to all my family and friends who have helped me along the way and encouraged me to succeed.

A special dedication to my son, Carlos. Momma loves you!

To my friend and author, Shuwanna White. Thank you for all your help and advice.

Most importantly, thank you to all my readers who are beautifully and wonderfully made! What I do is all for you! God bless you!

Juanese, LLC
Eads, TN

ISBN: 978-1-7357145-1-6

Animals are found everywhere
On land, in water or in the air
Some animals are big and some are small
Some have lots of legs; some have no legs at all
On the following pages you'll find a few
Of the animals I'd like to share with you....

Ants form colonies that range in size
Colonies are where ants live and survive

Butterflies come in many colors
They flap their wings and flutter, flutter, flutter

Cheetahs are known to run really fast
At least 70mph, they'll run right past!

Dolphins are found in the sea
They're smart and usually very friendly

Emus have long, thin necks and legs
Like other birds, they have babies by laying eggs

Fish have gills to help them breathe
And fins that help them swim with speed

Gerbils are popular to keep as pets
Rarely biting unprovoked or without stress

**Hedgehogs have stiff hairs called their spines
That resemble the quills of a porcupine**

Iguanas are lizards with excellent vision
To see shapes, colors and movement at distance

**Jellyfish are found in every ocean
For millions of years they've been in motion**

Kangaroos have large feet and powerful legs for leaping
The female keeps her baby in her pouch for safe-keeping

**Ladybugs are tiny and colorful, with spots
Most eat the insects that destroy farmers' crops**

Monkeys are also known as primates
They usually have tails, unlike the ape

Newts are aquatic; normally found in water
If you cut off their tails they'll grow another

Oysters can be found in an oyster reef
Some oysters make pearls and some oysters you eat

**Pandas live in China and like bamboo
You may be able to see one at the zoo**

Quolls are also called native cats
They have pink noses and fur that's brown or black

Roaches mainly like dark, and run from light
Some roaches have wings and will take flight

Snakes are elongated reptiles with no legs
That can usually swallow prey larger than their heads

Tarantulas are often hairy and very large spiders
Pet owners like the female 'cause her lifespan is higher

Urchins, or sea urchins, are spiny and round
Common colors include black, red, purple, green and brown

**Vultures have keen eyesight, muscular legs and sharp bills
These buzzards like to eat what's already been killed**

**Wasps have over a hundred-thousand species
And many are commonly mistaken for bees**

Xemes are Arctic gulls with a forked tail
That with boldness protects its young very well

**Yaks are heavily built with small ears and short legs,
Long shaggy hair, horns and a wide forehead**

Zebras are African horses with black and white stripes
When cornered they'll rear up and kick or bite

Illustration Contributor Page:

A - Alexandr Pakhnyushchyy @ 123RF.com

B - sunshinesmile @ 123RF.com

C - Eric Isselee @ 123RF.com

D - Golkin Oleg @ 123RF.com

E - Lyudmyla Raynard @ 123RF.com

F - vilainecrevette @ 123RF.com

G - Eric Isselee @ 123RF.com

H - Sergey Galushko @ 123RF.com

I - Adrienn Orbánhegyi @ 123RF.com

J - Dmitry Lobanov @ 123RF.com

K - kjuuurs @ 123RF.com

L - Anton Ignatenco @ 123RF.com

M - Tuomas Lehtinen @ 123RF.com

N - designpics @ 123RF.com

O - Josef Muellek @ 123RF.com

P - Stefano Tronci @ 123RF.com

Q - Susan Flashman @ 123RF.com

R - Mr.Smith Chetanachan @ 123RF.com

S - Eric Isselee @ 123RF.com

T - Globalphoto @ 123RF.com

U - Darryl Brooks @ 123RF.com

V - Alta Oosthuizen @ 123RF.com

W - paulrommer @ 123RF.com

X - Roy Longmuir @ 123RF.com

Y - Jakub Cejpek @ 123RF.com

Z - zixian @ 123RF.com

www.ingramcontent.com/pod-product-compliance
Lightning Source LLC
Chambersburg PA
CBHW060827270326
41931CB00002B/95